The Nature Kid's Guide to HYENAS

DAVID ANDERSON

LP Media Inc. Publishing
Text copyright © 2026 by LP Media Inc.

For information address LP Media Inc. Publishing,
30012 Variolite St NW, Princeton MN 55371
www.lpmedia.org

Publication Data

Hyenas
The Nature Kid's Guide to Hyenas — First edition.

Summary: "Learn all about Hyenas, the Nature Kid Way"
— Provided by publisher.

ISBN: 979-8-89818-211-3

[1. Hyenas – Non-Fiction] I. Title.

Title: The Nature Kid's Guide to Hyenas

CONTENTS

HOT HOME
DID YOU KNOW?
Hyenas are more closely related to cats than to dogs — but their closest relative is the mongoose!

Whooo! A hyena cries out across the hot, dry grass.

Hyenas live in some of the hottest places on Earth. They make their homes in grasslands and open plains. The sun beats down hard, but hyenas do not mind the heat.

These animals rest in dens during the day. A den can be a hole in the ground or a rocky cave. Inside, it stays cool even when temperatures outside climb past 100 degrees.

At night, hyenas come out to explore and play. The air is cooler then. That is when the real fun starts!

WORLD WIDE
FUN FACT!
Striped hyenas can survive in snowy mountain areas where temperatures drop below freezing!

Yip! A striped hyena trots through the desert sand.

Hyenas live in many parts of the world. You can find them in Africa, Asia, and the Middle East. Each type of hyena has adapted perfectly for their home.

Spotted hyenas roam the grasslands of Africa. Striped hyenas live in deserts and rocky hills. Brown hyenas stick to the coasts of southern Africa, where they search beaches for food.

Some hyenas live in forests. Others live near sandy dunes. From scorching deserts to misty coastlines, hyenas can make a home almost anywhere!

SIZE UP

FUN FACT!
A spotted hyena's head is so big and strong that it makes up almost one-third of its body weight!

Thud! A big spotted hyena lands hard on all four paws.

Spotted hyenas are the biggest type of hyena. They stand about 3 feet tall at the shoulder. A large one can weigh over 140 pounds!

Their front legs are longer than their back legs. This makes their back slope down toward the tail. It is a shape you would know anywhere!

The aardwolf is the smallest hyena. It weighs only about 20 pounds — less than most pet dogs. Unlike its fierce hyena cousins, the aardwolf eats almost nothing but termites!

BONE BREAKERS

Crunch! A hyena bites right through a thick, hard bone.

Hyenas have incredibly strong jaws. Their bite force can reach 1,100 pounds per square inch. They can crush bones that even lions cannot break, then digest them completely. Almost no other animal on Earth can do that!

Their hearts are unusually large for their body size, pumping enormous amounts of oxygen to their muscles. This gives hyenas almost endless energy for long chases across the savanna.

A hyena can eat up to a third of its own body weight in a single meal. Every part of this animal is built for one thing: surviving anything.

SUPER SNIFFERS

Sniff, sniff! A hyena picks up a scent miles away.

Hyenas have an amazing sense of smell. They can sniff out a dead animal from more than 2 miles away! Their big noses help them find meals even in total darkness.

Hyenas also hear very well. Their round ears turn like radar dishes to catch tiny sounds. They can hear other animals calling from far across the plains.

Their eyes are sharp too. Hyenas can see well in low light, which helps them hunt at night. All three senses working together make hyenas expert food finders.

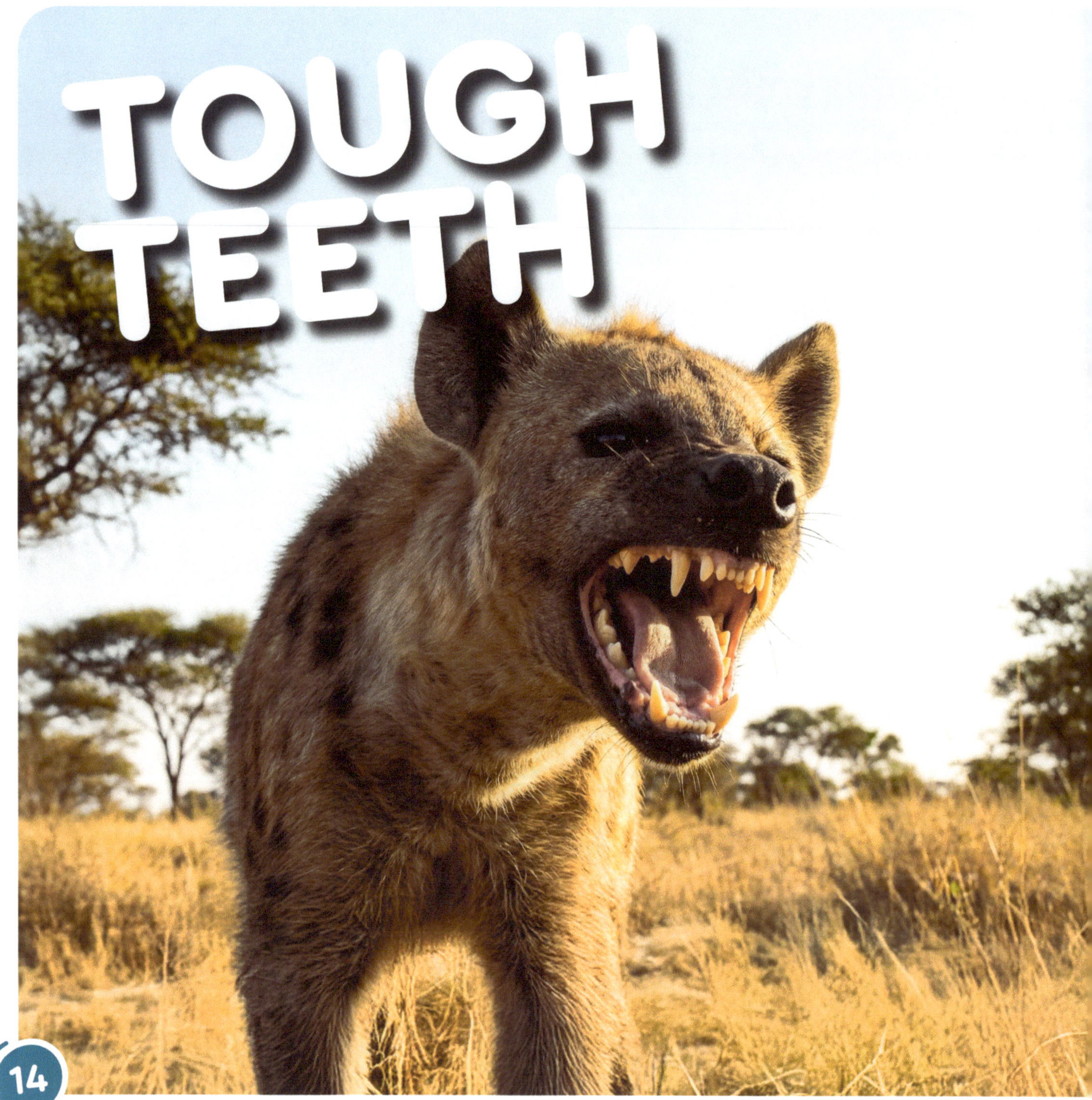
TOUGH
TEETH

Growl! A hyena shows its big teeth to scare a lion.

Hyenas are not easy to mess with. When danger is near, they show their sharp teeth. A flash of those big teeth scares most animals away!

Hyenas also puff up their fur to look bigger. They growl and make loud calls. This tells enemies to back off right now.

Their thick skin is hard to bite through. Even in a fight, hyenas are tough to hurt. They are built to take on trouble and win.

A hyena can heal from serious bites and wounds faster than almost any other mammal!

15

BONE BUFFET
DID YOU KNOW?
Hyenas can eat every part of their meal — even the teeth, hooves, and horns!
16

Chomp! A hungry brown hyena bites into a big, crunchy bone.

Hyenas eat almost anything. They munch on meat, bones, and even horns. Nothing goes to waste when a hyena eats!

Spotted hyenas hunt big animals like zebras and wildebeest. They also eat smaller prey like rabbits. When food is hard to find, they eat fruit and bugs too.

The brown hyena is different. It rarely hunts and instead searches for food that other animals left behind. It has the largest home range of any hyena, sometimes wandering over 25 miles in a single night just looking for its next meal!

PACK ATTACK

Spotted hyenas kill 95% of their own food — lions actually steal from hyenas more often than hyenas steal from lions!

Yowl! The hyena clan charges after a running zebra.

Spotted hyenas hunt in groups called clans. They work as a team to catch big prey. Together, they can take down animals much larger than themselves.

First, the clan picks out a weak or slow animal. Then they chase it as a group, taking turns at the front. This way, no one gets too tired.

Hyenas do not waste any food. After a catch, they eat fast. A hungry group can finish a whole zebra in just 15 minutes!

BIG BULLIES

Hyenas outnumber lions three to one across Africa, yet lions still win most face-to-face fights!

Roar! A big lion stomps over and tries to steal a meal.

Lions are the biggest threat to hyenas. They fight over food all the time. A big male lion is much stronger than any single hyena.

Wild dogs and leopards cause trouble too. They may try to hurt young hyenas when adults are away. Big birds like martial eagles sometimes swoop down to grab small cubs.

Life is not easy for hyenas. They face danger from many sides. But hyenas are some of the bravest animals around, and they never give up without a fight.

GANG GUARD

FUN
FACT!
A group of just six hyenas can
chase away a pride of lions!

Whoop! A hyena calls out and the whole clan comes running.

Hyenas stay safe by sticking together. When one hyena is in trouble, it calls out loud. The rest of the clan runs over to help right away.

A group of hyenas can scare away even a lion. They circle around and snap their powerful jaws. The more hyenas there are, the safer everyone feels.

Young hyenas stick close to the group for safety. Older hyenas keep watch for danger. Working together keeps the whole clan safe from harm.

FAST FEET

Hyenas can swim! They sometimes cross rivers and lakes to reach new hunting grounds.

Zoom! A spotted hyena sprints across the open plain.

Spotted hyenas are fast runners. They can reach speeds of 37 miles per hour! That is almost as fast as a car on a city street.

Hyenas can also run for a long time without stopping. They cover many miles chasing prey without getting tired. Their strong legs carry them easily over rough ground.

Hyenas have a bouncy trot that looks funny. They bob up and down as they run. But that goofy trot gets the job done every time!

NIGHT SHIFT

Hyenas greet their friends by sniffing and nuzzling — they can recognize over 100 different clan members by smell!

Rustle! At dusk a hyena stretches and steps out of its den.

Hyenas are most active at night. When the sun goes down, they come alive. The cool air makes it the perfect time to explore.

During the day, hyenas rest in shady spots. They nap under bushes or in tall grass. The hot sun makes them lazy and sleepy.

Once night comes, hyenas greet each other and set out together. They spend the night looking for food, patrolling their territory, and playing. When the sun rises, it is time to rest once more.

CLAN QUEENS

Yap! The hyena clan gathers around their fearless leader.

Spotted hyena clans are led by females. The top female is the boss. She makes the rules for the whole group!

A clan can have up to 80 hyenas living together. Every member has a rank. Some hyenas eat first, and some must wait until last.

Females are bigger and stronger than males. They make all the big choices for the clan. In the hyena world, girls run the show!

A hyena cub is born with the same rank as its mother — a low-ranking mom means a low-ranking cub!

LOVE LAUGHS

A hyena's famous laugh is really a sign that it is nervous, excited, or being pushed around by a higher-ranking hyena!

Hee-hee! A male hyena giggles to get a female's attention.

Male hyenas must work hard to find a mate. They bow and nod their heads. They also make soft sounds to show they are friendly and gentle.

The female picks the male she likes best. Males must be patient. Very patient! If a female says no, the male walks away quietly.

After mating, the male moves on. The female is now in charge of everything. She will soon get ready for new cubs.

CUTE CUBS

DID YOU KNOW?
Spotted hyena cubs are born jet black — they do not get their famous spots until they are a few months old!

Squeak! A tiny, dark hyena cub pops out of the den.

Hyena cubs are born in underground dens. Most mothers have two cubs at a time. The babies are small and weigh only about 3 pounds each.

Cubs can see and hear right from birth. They are born with their eyes wide open! This is different from puppies and kittens, who are born blind.

For the first weeks, cubs stay safe in the den. It is warm and dark inside. They cuddle close to mom, drink her milk, and grow fast.

MOM RULES

DID YOU KNOW?
Mother hyenas can tell their own cub's cry from dozens of other cubs — even in a noisy, crowded den!

Slurp! A hyena mother licks her tiny cub from head to toe.

Hyena mothers take care of their cubs all by themselves. Fathers do not help at all. Mom does everything on her own!

She feeds her cubs rich milk for over a year. Hyena milk has more protein and fat than almost any other land animal's milk. It helps the cubs grow big and strong.

Mothers also protect their babies from danger. If a predator comes close, mom fights back fiercely. No one messes with a hyena mom!

BORN TOUGH

DID YOU KNOW?
Hyenas can go several days without drinking any water — they get moisture from the food they eat!

Huff! A brown hyena trots through a cloud of hot, dry dust.

Hyenas are some of the toughest animals in Africa. They can live in places where food is hard to find. When times are tough, they eat whatever they can get.

Hyenas have strong bodies that can handle a lot. They stay healthy even in harsh places. Heat, dust, and hard times do not slow them down one bit.

These animals also adapt to changes quickly. If their home gets too dry, they move on to find water. Hyenas always find a way to survive.

ZOO SPOTS

You can tell spotted hyenas apart by their unique spot patterns — no two hyenas have the same spots!
FUN FACT!

38

Click! A pair of hyenas rest in their zoo enclosure.

You do not have to travel to Africa to see a hyena! Many zoos across the United States have spotted hyenas, and some even have brown hyenas and aardwolves too.

The best time to visit is early morning or late afternoon when hyenas are most active. Watch how they move, communicate, and interact with each other. You might even hear that famous laugh!

Many zoos have special programs where rangers share fun facts and answer questions. Learning about hyenas up close is the best way to truly appreciate these incredible animals.

GLOSSARY

territory

An area that an animal claims and defends from other animals

clan

A group of hyenas that live and work together

rank

An animal's place in the group order

dusk

The time of day just before it gets dark

savanna

A wide, open grassland with scattered trees, found mostly in Africa